SANTA MARIA PUBLIC LIBRARY

D0478634

j973.92092

Martin, Patricia Stone
    Ted Kennedy, Jr.: A Lifetime
of Challenges.

Discarded by
Santa Maria Library

BKM AUG 2 4 '92

CUY DEC 1 4 '92

BRANCH COPY
BOOKMOBILE

Ted Kennedy, Jr.
A Lifetime of Challenges

Patricia Stone Martin

illustrated by Karen Park

Rourke Enterprises Vero Beach, Florida

©1987 by Rourke Enterprises, Inc.

All rights reserved. No part of this book may be reproduced or utilized in any form or by any means, electronic or mechanical including photocopying, recording, or by any information storage and retrieval system without permission in writing from the publisher except for the inclusion of brief quotations in an acknowledged review.

Manufactured in the United States of America

Library of Congress Cataloging-in-Publication Data

Martin, Patricia Stone.
  Ted Kennedy, Jr. – a lifetime of challenges.

  (Reaching your goal biographies)
  Summary: A brief biography of Ted Kennedy, Jr., with emphasis on how he came to terms with the loss of a leg to cancer and his subsequent work with the disabled. Includes advice on setting and reaching goals.
    1. Kennedy, Edward Moore, 1961-   – Juvenile literature. 2. Kennedy, Edward Moore, 1932-   – Family – Juvenile literature. 3. Statesmen's children – United States – Biography – Juvenile literature. 4. Cancer – Patients – United States – Biography – Juvenile literature. [1. Kennedy, Edward Moore, 1961- 2. Physically handicapped] I. Title. II. Series: Martin, Patricia Stone. Reaching your goal biographies.
E840.8.K355M37 1987 973.92′092′4 [B] [92] 87-12126
ISBN 0-86592-174-1

Twelve-year-old Teddy was in bed. He did not want to be there. He wanted to be outside playing football or running. But on this cool November day, he had to stay indoors. He had a cold. He also had a large lump on his right leg just below the knee.

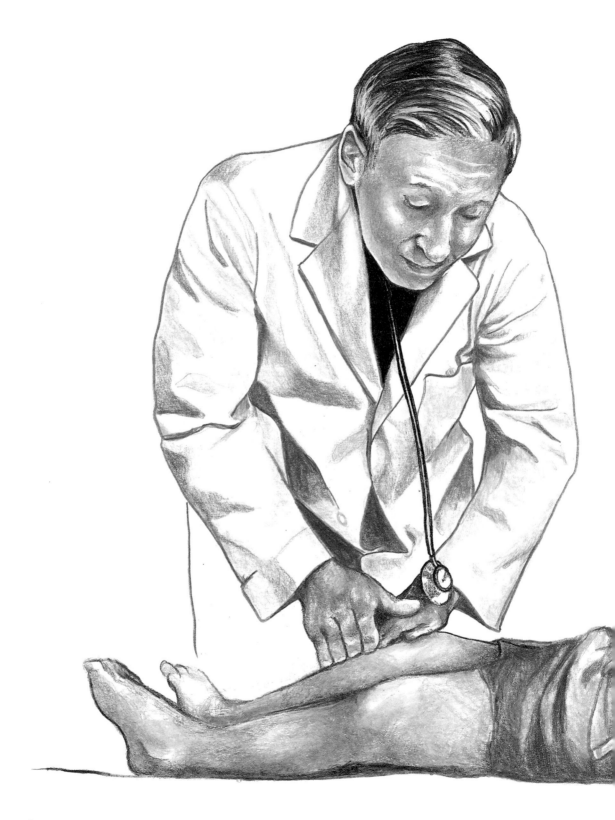

4

At first he thought he had hurt it playing football. But the lump had not gone away, and it hurt to walk. Finally his parents sent for a doctor. The doctor looked at the lump. He told Teddy's parents to watch it for two more days. If it did not go away, they should call him.

The lump did not go away. Teddy had to go to the hospital for tests. The tests showed that Teddy had cancer. His leg would have to be cut off above the knee. If they didn't do this, the cancer would spread.

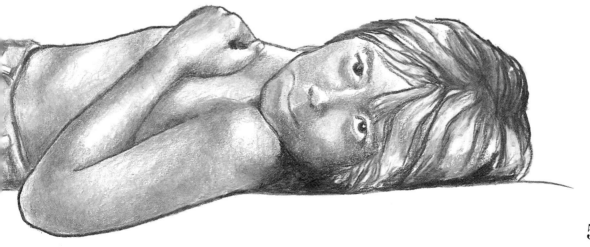

Teddy's father told him the bad news. He explained that the surgery would take place the next morning. Teddy was glad that he did not have to think about it for very long.

Teddy lost part of his leg, but he did not lose his courage. He decided to look on it as a challenge. He would face the challenge and win. And he has done just that.

Edward Moore Kennedy, Jr., was born on September 26, 1961, in Boston, Massachusetts. He was named after his father, who is also called Ted or Teddy. Teddy had a brother and a sister, and he grew up with many aunts, uncles and cousins nearby.

The Kennedy family is very wealthy. They are also famous. Teddy's father is a U.S. Senator. His uncle, John F. Kennedy, was president of the United States. Another uncle, Robert Kennedy, ran for president. Both uncles were assassinated, or killed. Almost everyone in the country has heard of the Kennedys.

President John F. Kennedy

Teddy's parents did not want their children to be spoiled. They taught them to be thankful for all the nice things they had. When they lost something they owned, they had to pay for it out of their own money.

Every summer, Teddy went sailing with his cousins. He loved to go camping and swimming. Once he rafted down the Colorado River with his father. He liked to play tennis. Every winter he skied at Sun Valley. Teddy had a fun and busy childhood.

Then came the day he had to lose his leg. Teddy's father and mother were with him. Teddy was afraid. He wondered why such a terrible thing was happening to him. The surgery took less than two hours. When Teddy woke up, his father was leaning over him.

Teddy held on tightly to his father. Teddy remembers thinking he might as well be dead. He did not want to go on living with only one leg.

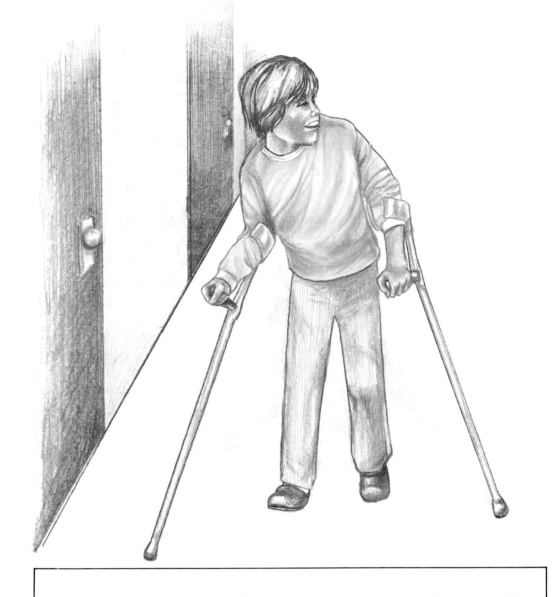

Teddy had to learn to do many things all over again. He was given an artificial leg. He had to learn to walk on it. At first, he was afraid to try. It hurt while he walked. He kept trying. By the end of the week, he could walk all the way down the hall by himself. After a while, his stump stopped hurting.

That Christmas, Teddy received hundreds of gifts from people he didn't know. He opened them all. He kept a few but gave most of them to a children's hospital. He wanted to make other children happy.

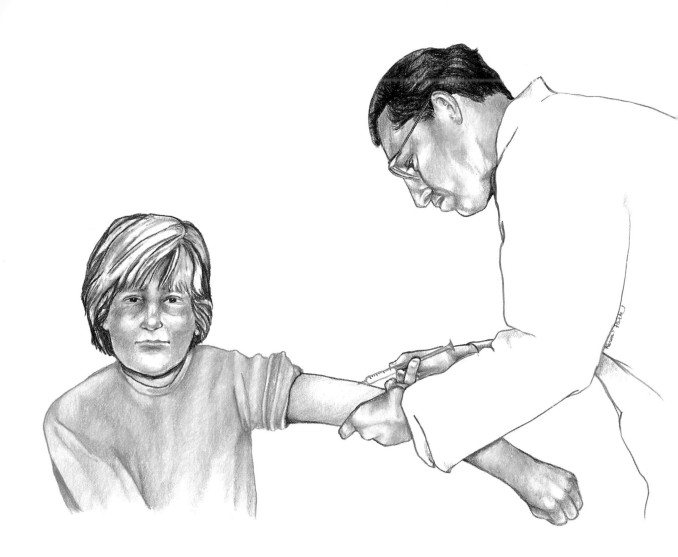

Teddy kept walking. In the beginning, he walked with a limp. Then the limp began to go away. To make sure the cancer would not return, Teddy had to have treatments. He had a series of shots every three weeks. The shots made him very sick.

Four months after the surgery, Teddy went skiing. His ski pole had two little skis on the end to help him stay up. One month after that, he went to Russia with his parents. That summer he flew to Ireland with five other boys. The next spring, Teddy went to Iran and Israel with his parents.

Then Teddy went to the doctor for a check-up. The news was good. The cancer had not come back! Teddy had been taking treatments for 18 months. Finally he did not need them anymore.

Teddy went back to school. Later he went to college. He became active in sports again. He loves to ski and has raced with other skiers who also have physical disabilities. He swims, boats, and even plays football.

Now Ted Kennedy, Jr., works to help other people who have disabilities. He talks to people in hospitals. He encourages people to accept their disabilities and work with them. He does not like the word *handicapped*. He prefers to say that these people are *challenged*. To be challenged means that you need to face something and overcome it. Ted faced living with only one leg. Other people have to face other challenges.

Ted has formed a group called Facing the Challenge. This group helps people with disabilities. We are all challenged in some way, Ted says. Some people can't see. Some people can't hear. Some people are shy. Some people have trouble reading or doing math.

Ted Kennedy, Jr., faced his challenge and won. He reached his goal. What is your challenge? Can you overcome it?

Reaching Your Goal

What are your goals? Here are some steps to help you reach them.

1. **Decide on your goal.**
   It may be a short-term goal like one of these:
   learning to ride a bike
   getting a good grade on a test
   keeping your room clean
   It may be a long-term goal like one of these:
   learning to read
   learning to play the piano
   becoming a lawyer

2. **Decide if your goal is something you really can do.**
   Do you have the talent you need?
   How can you find out? By trying!
   Will you need special equipment?
   Perhaps you need a piano or ice skates.
   How can you get what you need?
   Ask your teacher or your parents.

3. Decide on the first thing you must do.
   Perhaps this will be to take lessons.

4. Decide on the second thing you must do.
   Perhaps this will be to practice every day.

5. Start right away.
   Stick to your plan until you reach your goal.

6. Keep telling yourself, "I can do it!"

Good luck! You can face your challenge and win!

Reaching Your Goal Books

Beverly Cleary
She Makes Reading Fun

Bill Cosby Superstar

Jesse Jackson A Rainbow Leader

Ted Kennedy, Jr.
A Lifetime of Challenges

Christa McAuliffe
Reaching for the Stars

Dale Murphy
Baseball's Gentle Giant

Dr. Seuss We Love You

Samantha Smith Young Ambassador

Rourke Enterprises, Inc.
P.O. Box 3328
Vero Beach, FL 32964